The Essential Teachings of
Ramana Maharshi

A *Visual Journey*

The Essential Teachings of Ramana Maharshi

A *Visual Journey*

Edited by
Matthew Greenblatt

InnerDirections
PUBLISHING

InnerDirections Publishing

INNER DIRECTIONS FOUNDATION
P.O. Box 130070
Carlsbad, California 92013
Tel: 800 545-9118 • 760 599-4075
www.InnerDirections.org

SECOND EDITION
First edition published 2001
Second revised edition 2003

Cover and interior design by Joan Greenblatt & Chetna Bhatt

Printed in Canada

ISBN: 1-878019-18-X

Library of Congress Catalog Card Number: 2001092491

To know the truth of one's Self as the
sole Reality, and to merge and become
one with it, is the only true Realization.
—RAMANA MAHARSHI

Acknowledgments

This book came together as a labor of love. Primarily, we must thank Sri V.S. Ramanan, President of Sri Ramanasramam (the hermitage of Ramana Maharshi in Tiruvannamalai, South India). With his support, many special photos of Sri Ramana Maharshi have found their way into this book.

The printing of the first edition was made possible by the generous assistance of Dr. V.A. Ram and Mrs. Girijamma Ram (Las Vegas), who have supported this effort in the loving memory of their late son, Surya Paul Ram.

Special thanks must also go to Dr. Robert Powell, who assisted in the selection of quotes, and to Ronald S. Miller and Phyllis Kahaney, who served as editorial consultants.

Foreword

I have to record my gratitude to Maharshi for his insistence on the ever-present accessibility, the naturalness, the obviousness, of Self-realization. Many a time, I had been informed and had read, that Enlightenment is, of all states, the rarest and the remotest and the most difficult—in practice, impossible—and here was a great sage telling us that, on the contrary, it was the easiest. Such, indeed, was my own experience, and I had never been intimidated by those religious persons who were careful to tell me that I couldn't see what I saw. Nevertheless, for me it was marvelously refreshing to find that Maharshi never sent inquirers away with instructions to work for Liberation at some distant date. It is not, he insisted, a glittering prize to be awarded for future achievements of any sort; it is not for earning little by little, but for noticing now, just as one is. Other sages, of course, have stressed the availability of this, but here Maharshi is surely the clearest, the most uncompromising of them all. How wonderful to hear him saying, in effect, that compared with Oneself all other things are obscure, more or less invisible, fugitive, impossible to get at; only the Seer can be clearly seen.

I thank him for his uncompromising attitude to people's problems. For him, all the troubles that afflict humans reduce to one trouble—mistaken identity. The answer to the problem is to see "Who" has it. At its own level it is insoluble. And it must be so. There is no greater absurdity, no more fundamental or damaging a madness, than to imagine one is centrally what one looks like. To think one is a human being limited to this perspective is a sickness so deep-seated that it underlies and generates all one's ills. Only cure that one basic disease—mistaken identity—and all is exactly as it should be. I know no sage who goes more directly to the root of the disease and refuses more consistently to treat its symptoms. WHO AM I? is the only serious question. And, most fortunately, it is the only question that can be answered without hesitation or the shadow of a doubt, absolutely.

I thank Ramana Maharshi above all for tirelessly posing this question of questions, for showing how simple the answer is, and for his lifelong dedication to that simple answer.

Douglas E. Harding
Nacton, England

Introduction

This book presents the essential teachings of Sri Ramana Maharshi in a free-flowing, easy-to-read format. It is not meant to provide a comprehensive anthology of the teachings of this beloved sage. We have taken great care to preserve the integrity of Sri Ramana's words, while occasionally modifying some passages to reflect contemporary English usage.

A Note on the Teachings

All human beings search for an unending source of peace and happiness. Some of us turn to religion or philosophy in an effort to find the key, others turn to repeated experiences of enjoyment, while many take comfort in building a financial safety net. In the end, we all desire the same goal: to experience enduring happiness.

The many philosophical methods and religious teachings that promise true peace and happiness generally emphasize a "goal" and an "individual" who must attain it. They also often recommend various methods to improve oneself in order to reach that goal. The common denominator throughout these various means is the "individual" who approaches the Divine, the Absolute, Consciousness (whatever name we wish to call it) to gain that state of unending peace.

The teachings of Sri Ramana Maharshi help us see firsthand "who" and "what" our true identity is. They reveal at the most profound level the very nature of such a search and its final outcome. Only when we have tasted the peace and joy of our essential Being does the nature of Reality become clear. We begin to see clearly that there is really nothing to improve, nothing to become, and nothing to change. Our true nature is perfect right now and always has been.

The challenge before us, then, is not one of self-improvement—to make a better "me." Rather, it is to stop identifying with the psychological impressions and erroneous beliefs that keep us from seeing ourselves as we truly are. In other words, what we generally know about "I" is really only limited, secondhand knowledge, processed through the filter of the mind and senses.

Ramana Maharshi's philosophy—if one can even call it that—offers a roadmap to our true Self. He asks us to see through firsthand experience that the objective world has no reality apart from our own Being. In fact, there is no "objective" reality at all. His teachings have grown in popularity and esteem precisely because they offer a clear, direct means to perceive That—which is eternal and infinite—without a religious or conventional spiritual context.

The term Ramana used to describe the full awakening to our true nature is "Self-realization." By Self, he refers to the fundamental nature of all beings, the One Reality. The Self is the basis of all, the substrate of the individual that is identical with the Absolute (*Brahman*). In describing our true nature, Ramana has chosen an ideal term, for what can be nearer than one's Self?

Maharshi says that forgetfulness of our true nature as the Self gives rise to the "I"-sense. We then speculate about God as a Supreme Being instead of experiencing it directly. Although speculation and discussion prove intellectually stimulating, we can only *know* for certain about our true nature through the direct experience of Reality. In the end, all religious and spiritual teachings need to answer this question of identity. So, asks Ramana, why not begin from this very point? As he states,

> "Whatever be the means adopted, you must at last return to the Self; so why not abide in the Self here and now?"

Self-realization does not involve gaining any kind of intellectual knowledge or adopting a particular set of beliefs. "Self-realization," says Ramana, "is not knowing anything or becoming anything." It is simply a state of *Being*, our inherently natural state. Since the mind is only an instrument of the Self, it can never know its true source. Consequently, one can only *be* That.

Ramana Maharshi's teachings reflect the philosophical viewpoint of *advaita* (not-two). This profound view of the nature of Reality removes the distinction between subject and object, seer and seen, one's self and the world. To the awakened sage, the world is none other than the Self.

Advaita, or nonduality, is neither a philosophy nor a way of life. It is simply being "One without a second," as the *Upanishad* states. In truth, there can be no separate existence from the ever-present Reality. As Maharshi points out, what we search for is always within our reach:

> "The Real is ever as it is. All we have to do is give up regarding the unreal as real."

By persistently investigating the nature of the "I," we begin to see its unstable and fickle nature. As we steadfastly pursue this self-inquiry, the experience of "I," which we have so long believed to be true, begins to subside, and the universal "I," which is who we truly are, reveals itself for what it has always been. This is the true spiritual rebirth. As we begin to identify with the Universal "I," the Self, we also start to live in a state free from ego-based ideas and concepts. We see that the immediate experience of our own Being is the screen upon which all of life's events take place. Moreover, abiding peace and happiness, which we elusively sought before, arise spontaneously as our very Self.

Ramana Maharshi continually asks us to return to the Source of our true Being. The simple and direct approach he taught eliminates the need to undertake a path of self-improvement, since wherever we go, the Self is always present. There are no special requirements for investigating "who we really are," but he reminds us that earnestness of purpose certainly facilitates the opening of our hearts to the infinite Self.

A Brief Biography

In the ancient township of Tiruchulli, in a dry, dusty corner of South India, Venkataraman was born. Though destined to become one of the great sages of our time, there were no obvious signs that would foretell his realization.

After young Venkataraman's father passed away, the family moved to the temple town of Madurai to live with an uncle. Shortly after this time, Venkataraman faced his own mortality. One day, when all of the family members were away from home, the young boy (now sixteen years old) was overcome with an intense fear of death. Rather than panic

The mind is nothing but the thought "I."

Thoughts arise because of the thinker.

*The thinker is the ego, which if sought
will automatically vanish.*

Without Consciousness, time and space do not exist; they appear within Consciousness but have no reality of their own.

It is like a screen on which all this is cast as pictures and move as in a cinema show.

The Absolute Consciousness alone is our real nature.

Grace is within you;
Grace is the Self.

Grace is not something to be acquired from others.
If it is external, it is useless. All that is necessary
is to know its existence in you.

You are never out of its operation.

The mind cannot seek the mind.

You ignore what is real and hold on to
that which is unreal, then try to find
what it is. You think you are the
mind and, therefore, ask how it
is to be controlled.

If the mind exists, it
can be controlled, but it
does not. Understand
this truth by
inquiry.

Seek the real, the Self.

The Eternal is not born nor does it die.

We confound appearance with Reality. Appearance carries its end in itself.

What is it that appears anew?

If you cannot find it, surrender unreservedly to the substratum of appearances; then Reality will be what remains.

Reality is simply loss of the ego.

Destroy the ego by seeking its identity.

Because the ego has no real existence, it will automatically
vanish, and Reality will shine forth by itself in all its glory.
This is the direct method.

All other methods retain the ego. In those paths so many
doubts arise, and the eternal question remains to be tackled.
But in this method the final question is the only one and
is raised from the very beginning.

No practices (*sadhanas*) are even
necessary for this quest.

Your duty is to Be,
and not to be this
or that.

"I Am That I Am" sums up the
whole truth; the method is
summarized in
"Be Still."

The state we call Realization is simply being one's self, not knowing anything or becoming anything.

If one has realized, one is that which alone is and which alone has always been. One cannot describe that state, but only be That. Of course, we loosely talk of Self-realization for want of a better term.

There is no help in changing
your environment.

The obstacle is the mind, which must be overcome,
whether at home or in the forest. If you can do it in the
forest, why not in the home? Therefore,
why change the environment?

The cause of misery is not in life without; it is within you as the ego.

*You impose limitations on yourself and then make a
vain struggle to transcend them.*

Why attribute to the happenings in life the cause of misery, which
really lies within you? What happiness can you get from anything
extraneous to yourself? When you get it, how long will it last?

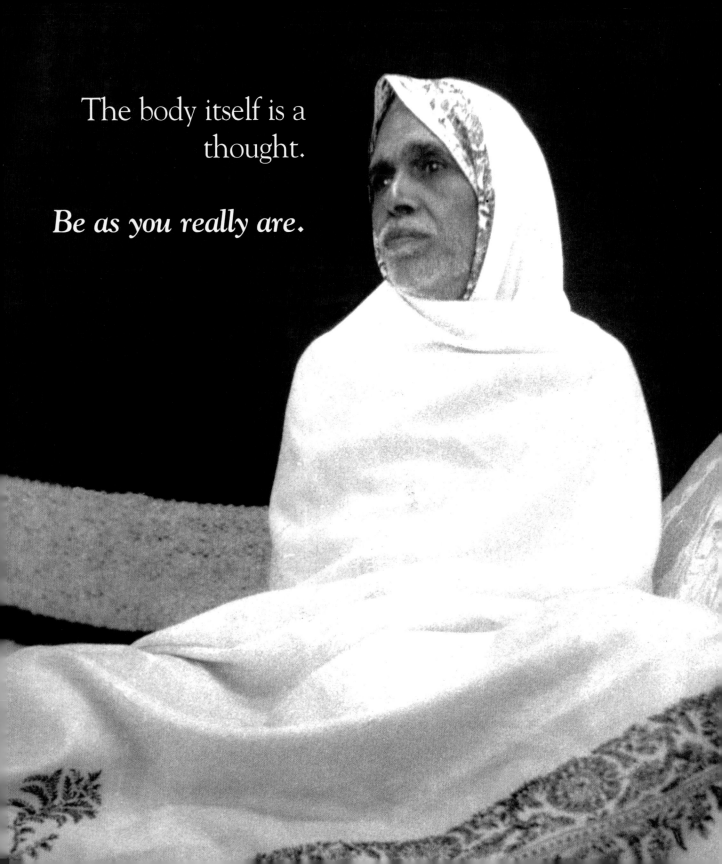

The body itself is a
thought.

Be as you really are.

There are no stages in Realization or degrees of Liberation.

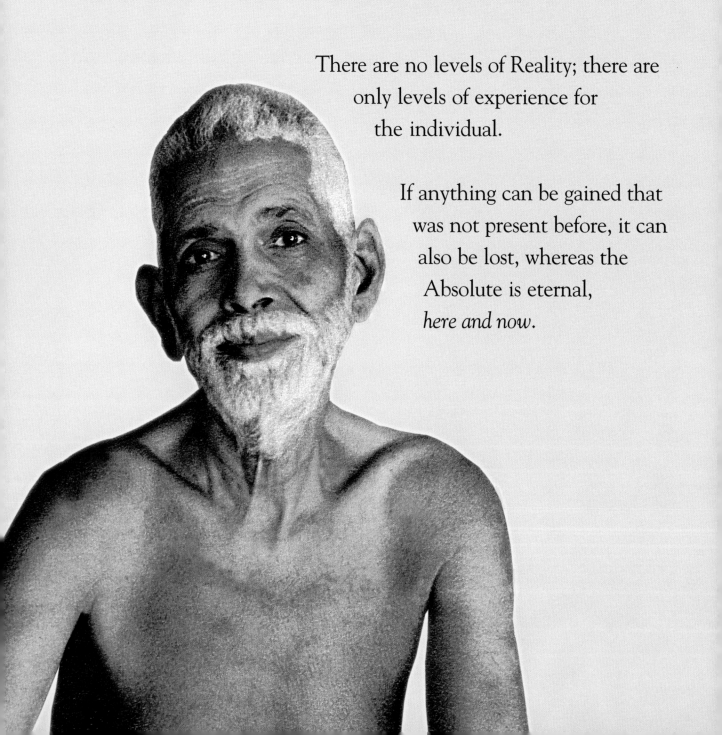

There are no levels of Reality; there are only levels of experience for the individual.

If anything can be gained that was not present before, it can also be lost, whereas the Absolute is eternal, *here and now.*

It is not a matter of becoming
but of Being.

Remain aware of yourself
and all else will be known.

One comes into existence for
a certain purpose.

That purpose will be accomplished
whether one considers oneself
the actor or not.

Everything is
predetermined.

But one is always free not to
identify oneself with the
body and not to be
affected by the
pleasure and pain
associated with
its activities.

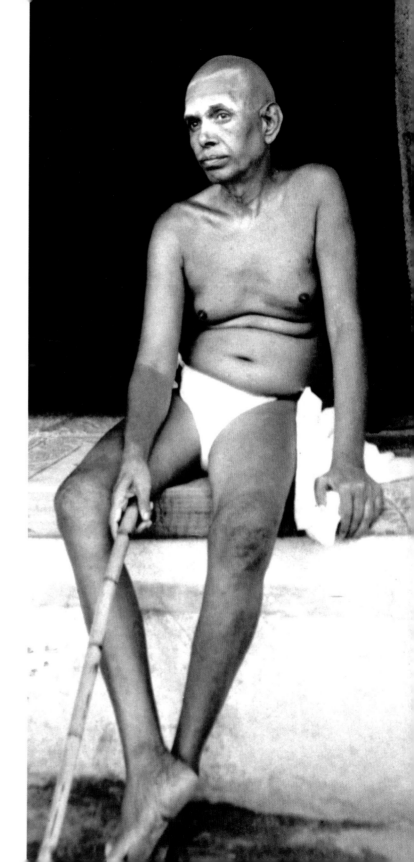

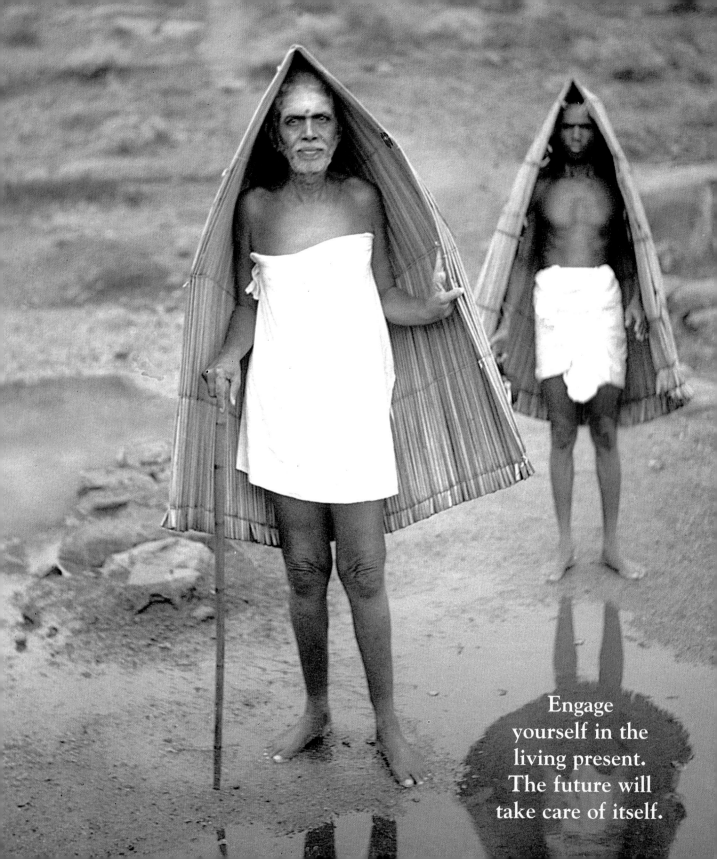

Engage
yourself in the
living present.
The future will
take care of itself.

Find out who is subject to free will or predestination and abide in that state.

Then both are transcended.
That is the only purpose in discussing
these questions. To whom do such questions
present themselves?

Discover that and be at peace.

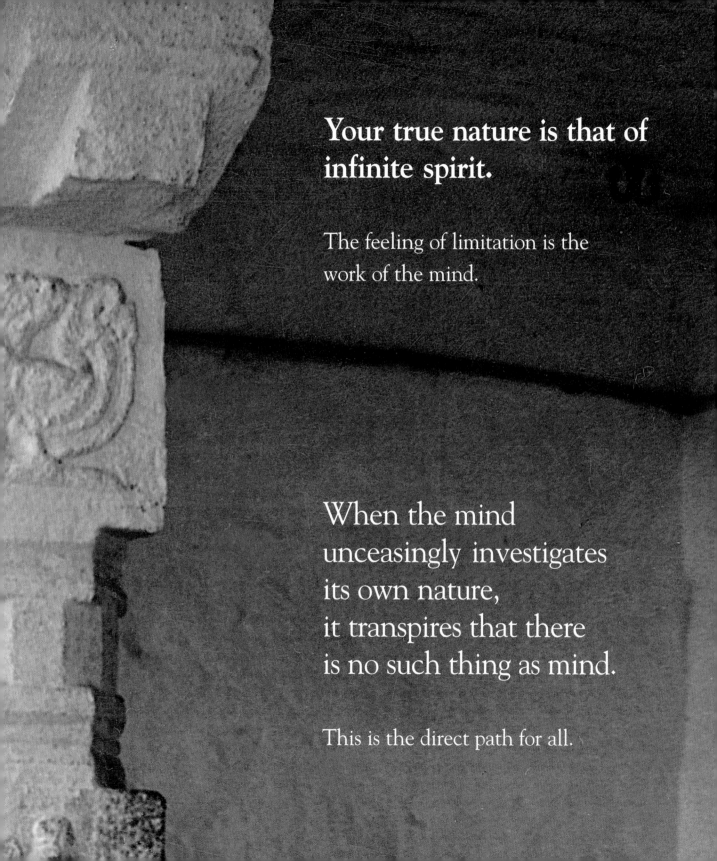

Your true nature is that of infinite spirit.

The feeling of limitation is the work of the mind.

When the mind
unceasingly investigates
its own nature,
it transpires that there
is no such thing as mind.

This is the direct path for all.

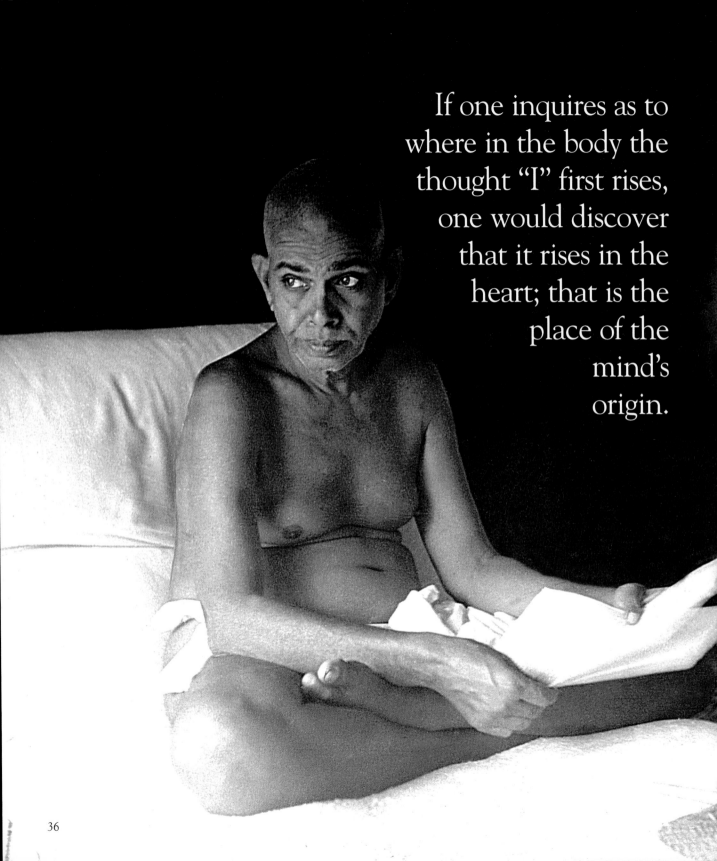

If one inquires as to where in the body the thought "I" first rises, one would discover that it rises in the heart; that is the place of the mind's origin.

Grace is always present.

You imagine it is something somewhere high in the sky, far away, and has to descend. It is really inside you, in your Heart, and the moment you effect subsidence or merger of the mind into its Source, grace rushes forth, sprouting as from a spring within you.

You speak as if you
are here, and the
Self is somewhere
else and you had
to go and
reach it . . .

... But in fact the Self is here
and now, and you are always It.

It is like being here and asking people
the way to the ashram, then
complaining that each
one shows a different
path and asking
which to
follow.

The realized person weeps with the weeping,
laughs with the laughing, plays with
the playful, sings with
those who sing,
keeping time
to the song.

What does he lose?

His presence is like a pure, transparent mirror.
It reflects our image exactly as we are.
It is we who play the several parts in life and reap the
fruits of our actions. How is the mirror or the stand on which it is
mounted affected? Nothing affects them, as they are mere supports.

The Consciousness of
"I" is the subject of all our actions.

Inquiring into the true nature of that
Consciousness and remaining as oneself
is the way to understand
one's true nature.

All that is required
to realize the Self
is to *Be Still.*

What can be
easier than that?

If one gains the **Peace of the Self, it will spread without any effort** on the part of the individual.

When one is not peaceful, oneself, how can one spread peace in the world?

Unless one is happy, one cannot bestow happiness on others.

Happiness is born of Peace and can reign
only when there is no disturbance.
Disturbance is due to thoughts, which
arise in the mind. When the mind
is absent there will be
perfect Peace.

Reality lies beyond the mind.

So long as the mind functions,
there is duality. Once it is transcended,
Reality shines forth.

Self-effulgence is the Self.

Satsang means association (*sanga*)
with Being (*Sat*), which is
the Self.

For whom is association?

The ultimate truth is so simple;
it is nothing more than being
in one's natural,
original state.

It is a great wonder that to teach such a simple truth
a number of religions should be necessary,
and so many disputes should go on
between them as to which is
the God-ordained teaching.
What a pity!

Just be the Self, that is all.

Because people want something elaborate and mysterious, so many religions have come into existence. Only those who are mature can understand the matter in its naked simplicity.

There is neither past nor future; there is only the present.

Yesterday was the present when you experienced it; tomorrow will also be the present when you experience it.

Therefore, experience takes place
only in the present, and beyond
and apart from experience
nothing exists.

Even the present
is mere imagination,
for the sense of time is purely mental.

Because people love mystery and not the truth, religions cater to them, eventually bringing them around to the Self.

Whatever be the means adopted, you must at last return to the Self; so why not abide in the Self here and now?

There is no greater mystery than this:
Being Reality ourselves, we seek
to gain Reality.

We think that there is
something hiding Reality
and that it must be
destroyed before
the truth is gained.
This is clearly ridiculous.

A day will dawn when you
will laugh at your past efforts.
*What you realize on the
day you laugh is also
here and now.*

If we look upon the Self as the ego, we become the ego, if as the mind we become the mind, if as the body we become the body.

It is thought that builds up layers in so many ways.

Take no notice of the ego and its activities but see only the light behind it.

The ego is the
"I"-thought.

The true
"I" is the Self.

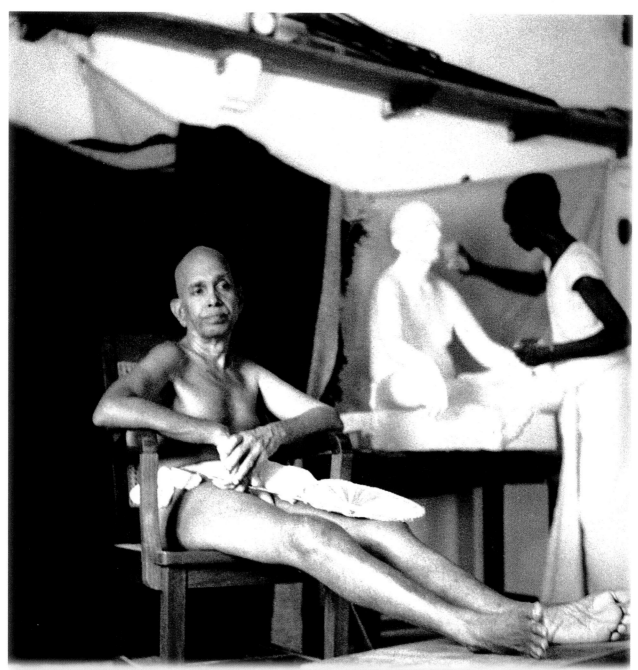

The world does not exist in sleep and forms a projection of your mind in the waking state. *It is therefore an idea and nothing else.*

It is false to speak of Realization;
what is there to realize?

The real is ever as it is.

All that is required is to cease
regarding as real that which is unreal.
That is all we need to attain
wisdom (*jnana*).

The universe is only an object created by the mind and has its being in the mind. It cannot be measured as an external entity.

The world phenomena, within or without, are only fleeting and are not independent of our Self.

Only the habit of looking at them as real and located outside ourselves is responsible for hiding our pure Being.

When the ever-present sole Reality, the Self, is found,
all other unreal things will disappear,
leaving behind the knowledge
that they are not other
than the Self.

Either surrender
because you realize
your inability and
need a higher power
to help you, or
investigate the cause
of misery.

The Divine never
forsakes one who has
surrendered.

60

To identify oneself with the body
and yet seek happiness is like
attempting to cross a river
on the back of an
alligator.

In truth, you are Spirit.

The body has been projected by the
mind, which itself originates from
Spirit. If the wrong identification
ceases, there will be peace and
permanent, indescribable bliss.

Those who
have realized
the Self, which
is the ground
of fate and
free will, are
free from them.

Ramana's reply to his mother, when she requested that he return home with her:

The Ordainer controls the fate of souls in accordance with their destiny (*prarabdha karma*). Whatever is destined not to happen will not happen, try as you may. Whatever is destined to happen will happen, do what you may to prevent it. This is certain.

The best course, therefore, is to remain silent.

The real state must be effortless.
It is permanent.

Efforts are spasmodic and so also are their results.

When your real, effortless, joyful
nature is realized, it will not
be inconsistent with the
ordinary activities
of life.

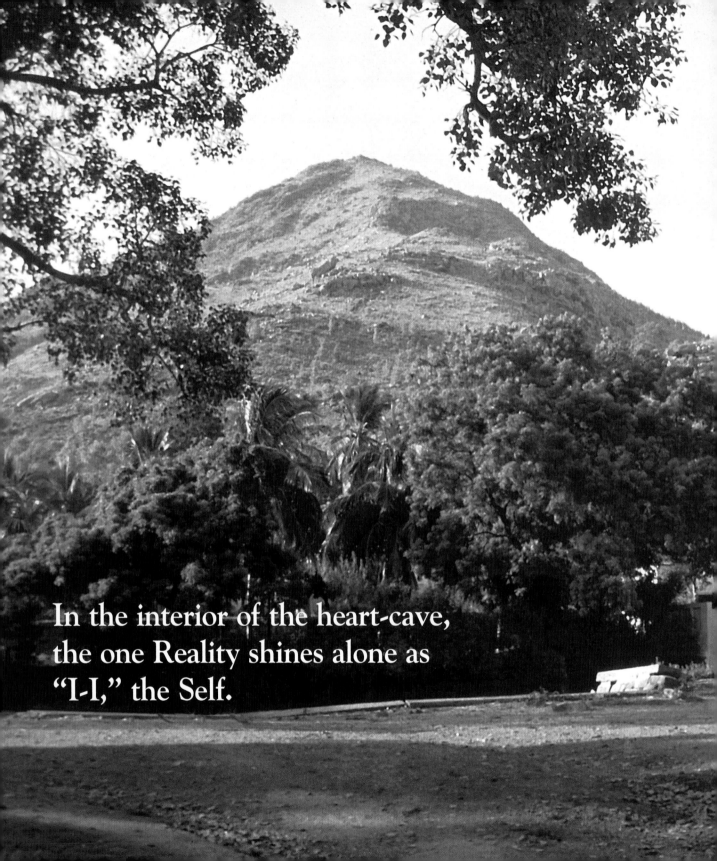

In the interior of the heart-cave,
the one Reality shines alone as
"I-I," the Self.

The Heart is the only Reality.

The mind is only a transient phase.
To remain as one's Self is to enter the Heart.

Apart from thought, there is no independent entity called "world."

In deep sleep, there are no thoughts and there is no world. In waking and dreaming, there are thoughts, and there is a world, also.

Just as the spider emits the thread (of the web) out of itself and then withdraws it, likewise, the mind projects the world out of itself and then withdraws it back into itself.

The Self is
all-pervading.

Therefore, no particular place
can be allocated for leading a life of
solitude.

To abide in the tranquil state that is
devoid of thought is to lead a life of
solitude and seclusion.

When your standpoint becomes that of wisdom, you will find the world to be God.

The question is one of outlook.

The universe exists within the Self.

Therefore, it is real, but only because it obtains its reality from the Self. We call it unreal, however, to indicate its changing appearance and transient form, whereas we call the Self real because it is changeless.

We see only the script and not the paper on which the script is written.

The paper is there, whether the script is on it or not. To those who look upon the script as real, you have to say that it is unreal—an illusion—since it rests upon the paper.

The wise person looks upon both paper and script as one.

Our real nature is Liberation,
but we imagine that we are bound . . .

. . . we make strenuous efforts to become free, although all the while we are free.

A person goes to sleep in this hall and dreams he has gone on a world-tour, traveling over various continents. After many years of strenuous travel, he returns to this county, enters the ashram, and walks into the hall.

Just at that moment, he wakes up and finds that he has not moved at all but has been sleeping. He has not returned after great efforts to this hall, but was here all the time.

If it is asked, "Why, being free, we imagine ourselves bound?" I answer, "Why, being in the hall, did you imagine you were on a world tour, crossing desert and sea?"

It is all mind.

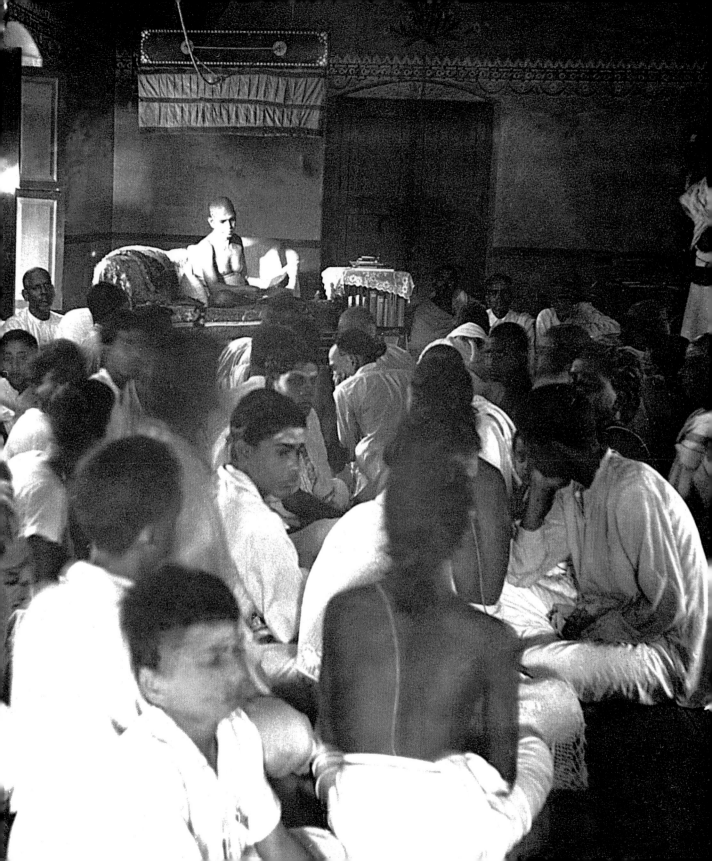

*With a smile, Ramana placed his
little finger over his eye and said:*

Look. This little finger
covers the eye and prevents
the whole world from
being seen. In the same
way this small mind
covers the whole
universe and
prevents Reality
from being seen.

See how
powerful
it is!

80

What *is*, is the Self. It is all-pervading.

We fill the mind with all sorts of impressions and then say
there is no room for the Self in it.

If all the false ideas and impressions are swept away and thrown
out, what remains is a feeling of fullness, which is the Self.
Then there will be no such thing as
a separate "I."

Meditation
on the Self,
which is oneself,
is the greatest of all
meditations.

All other meditations
are included in this.

*True silence is
really endless speech.*

There is no attaining it
because it is always present.

All you have to do is remove
the coverings that
conceal it.

Surrender is giving oneself up to the origin of one's Being.

In due course, we will know that our glory lies where we cease to exist.

The pet squirrel is waiting
for an opportunity to run out of its cage.

Ramana remarks:

All want to rush out.
There is no limit to
going out. Happiness
lies within and
not without.

All spiritual teachings are only
meant to make us retrace
our steps to our
Original Source.

We need not acquire anything new, only give
up false ideas and useless accretions.

Instead of doing this, we try to grasp something
strange and mysterious because we believe happiness
lies elsewhere. This is the mistake.

Forgetfulness of your real
nature is true death;
remembrance of
it is rebirth.

What appears will also disappear and is therefore impermanent. The Self never appears and disappears and is therefore permanent.

It is the only Reality.

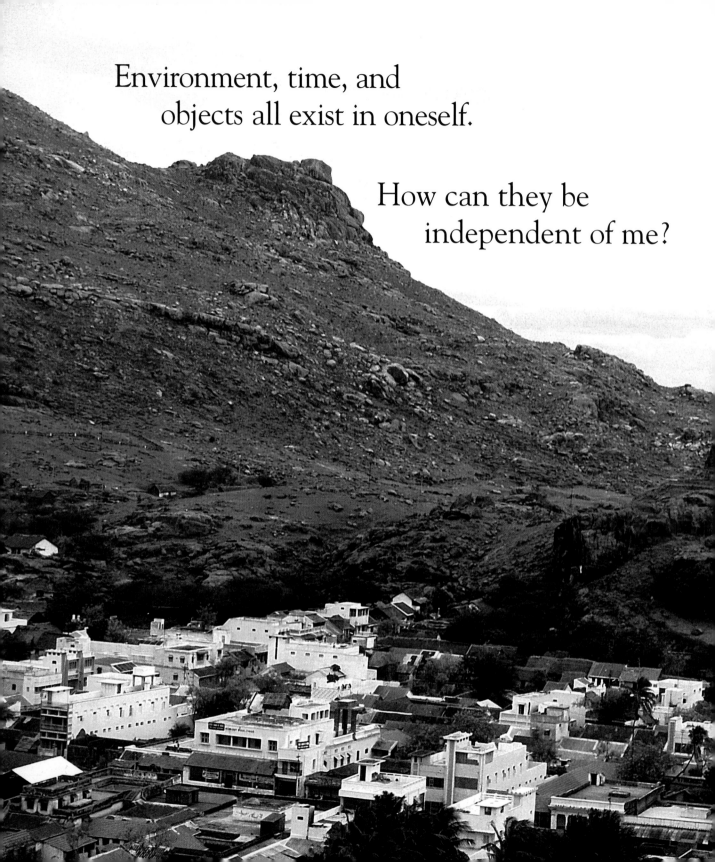

Environment, time, and
    objects all exist in oneself.

            How can they be
                independent of me?

They may change, but "I" remain unchanging.

Make no effort either to work or to
give up work; your very effort
is the bondage.

What is destined to happen will happen. Leave it to the
Higher Power; you cannot renounce or
retain as you choose.

The feeling "I work" is the hindrance.

Ask yourself, "Who works?" Remember who you are.
Then the work will not bind you;
it will proceed automatically.

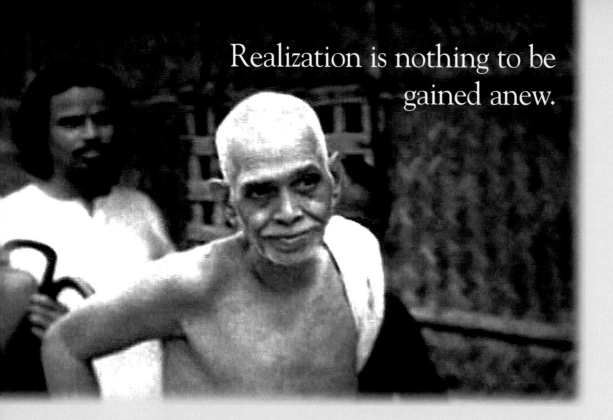

Realization is nothing to be gained anew.

You are the Self.
You are already and eternally That.

*There is never a moment when
the Self is not; it is ever-present,
here and now.*

If Realization were something to be gained hereafter, there
would be an equal chance of its being lost; this cannot
be Liberation, which is eternal.

Realization consists
of getting rid of the
false idea that one is
not realized.

What is called
"mind" is a wondrous
power residing in the
Self.

It causes all thoughts to arise.
Apart from thoughts, there is
no such thing as mind.
Therefore, thought
is the nature
of mind.

Self-inquiry directly leads to Self-realization by removing the obstacles which make you think that the Self is not already realized.

It reveals the truth that neither the ego nor the mind really exists and enables one to realize the pure, undifferentiated Being, which is the Self or the Absolute.

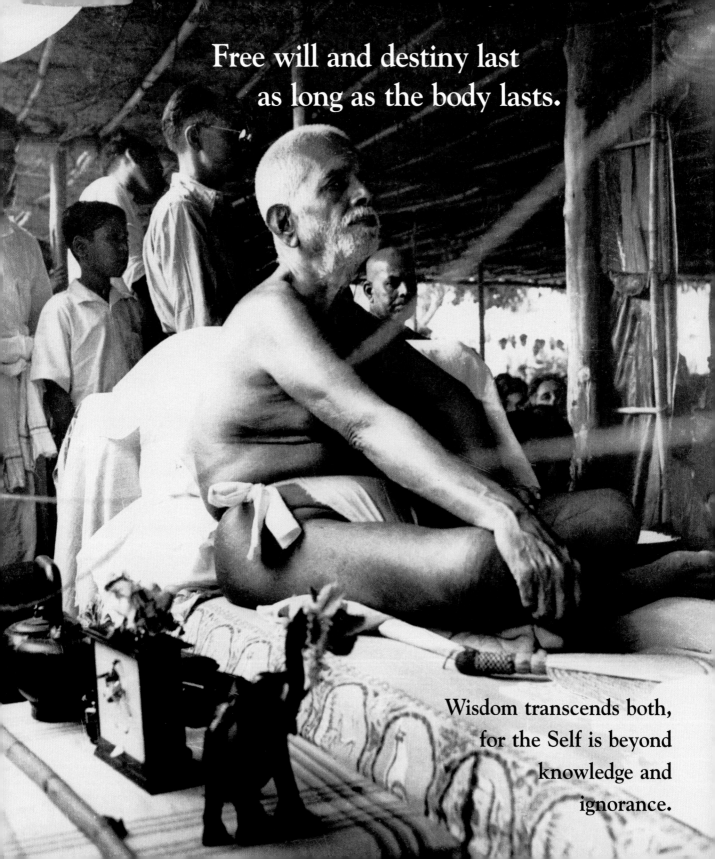

Free will and destiny last
as long as the body lasts.

Wisdom transcends both,
for the Self is beyond
knowledge and
ignorance.

Pain or pleasure is the result of past
actions and not of the present . . .
they alternate with each other.

One must always try to abide in the Self and
not be swayed by the pain or pleasure met
with occasionally.

*One who is indifferent to pain or pleasure
can alone be happy.*

Thoughts
change
but not
you.

Thoughts form your bondage and are not external to
you, so no external remedy need be sought for freedom.

What does it matter
if the mind is active?
It is only so on the
substratum of the
Self.

Hold to the
Self even
during mental
activity.

The "I" casts off the illusion of "I" and yet remains as "I."

Such is the paradox of Self-realization.

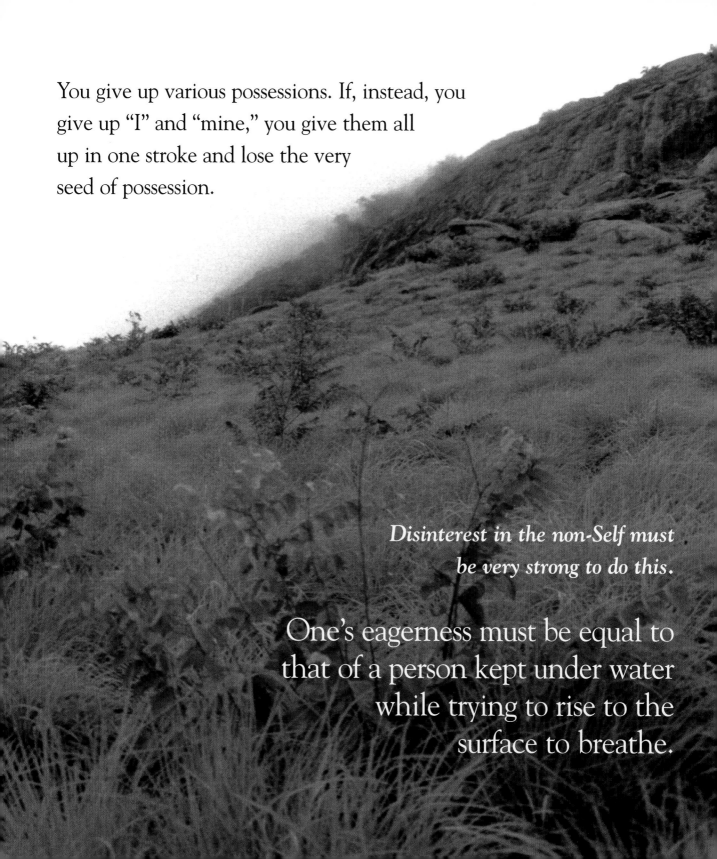

You give up various possessions. If, instead, you give up "I" and "mine," you give them all up in one stroke and lose the very seed of possession.

Disinterest in the non-Self must be very strong to do this.

One's eagerness must be equal to that of a person kept under water while trying to rise to the surface to breathe.

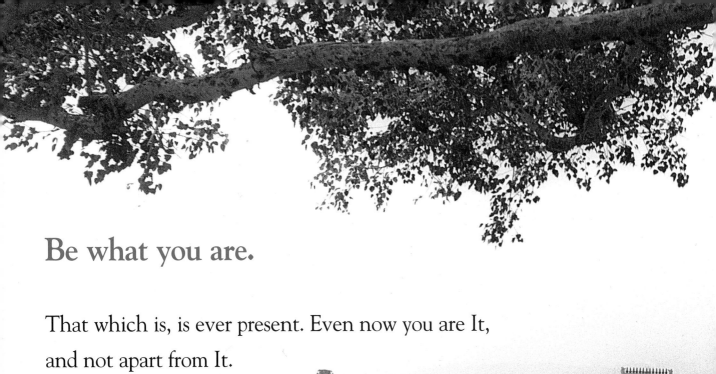

Be what you are.

That which is, is ever present. Even now you are It,
and not apart from It.

The expectation to see and the desire to get
something are all the working of the ego.

Be yourself and nothing more.

Pleasure or pain are only aspects of the mind. Our essential nature is happiness.

We forget the Self and imagine the body
or the mind to be the Self. It is this
wrong identity that gives rise to misery.

Happiness is
inherent in
everyone
and
is not due
to external
causes.

Because you have lost hold of the Self, thoughts afflict you; you see the world and doubts arise, along with anxiety about the future.

There is no use removing doubts.

If we clear one doubt, another arises, and there will be no end of doubts. All doubts will cease only when the doubter and his source have been found. Seek for the source of the doubter, and you find he is really nonexistent.

Doubter ceasing, doubts will cease.

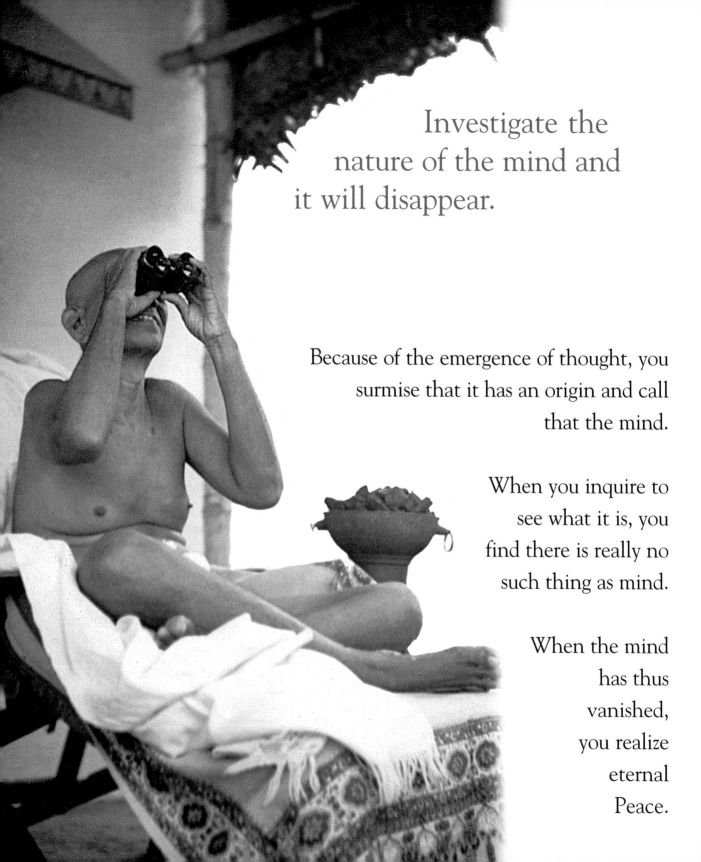

Investigate the
nature of the mind and
it will disappear.

Because of the emergence of thought, you
surmise that it has an origin and call
that the mind.

When you inquire to
see what it is, you
find there is really no
such thing as mind.

When the mind
has thus
vanished,
you realize
eternal
Peace.

When the mind, turning inward, inquires, "Who am I?" and reaches the heart, that which is "I" (the ego) sinks crestfallen, and the One (Self) appears of its own accord as "I-I." Though it appears thus, it is not the ego; it is the Whole.

It is the real Self.

The Self is free from all qualities.

Good or bad qualities
pertain only to
the mind.

The numeral one gives rise to other numbers.
The truth is neither one nor two.

It is as it is.

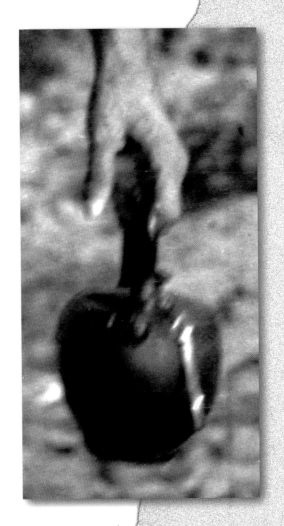

Dvaita and *advaita* are relative terms. They are based on a sense of duality. There is actually neither *dvaita* nor *advaita*.

I Am That I Am . . .

Simple Being is the Self.

The limited and multifarious thoughts having disappeared, there shines in the Heart a kind of wordless illumination of "I-I," which is pure Consciousness.

If one remains quiet without abandoning
that understanding, then egoity—the
individual sense of the form "I-am-
the-body"—will be totally destroyed.
And ultimately, the final thought,
the "I"-thought, will also be
extinguished, like camphor
that is burned by fire.

The great sages and scriptures
declare that this alone is
Realization.

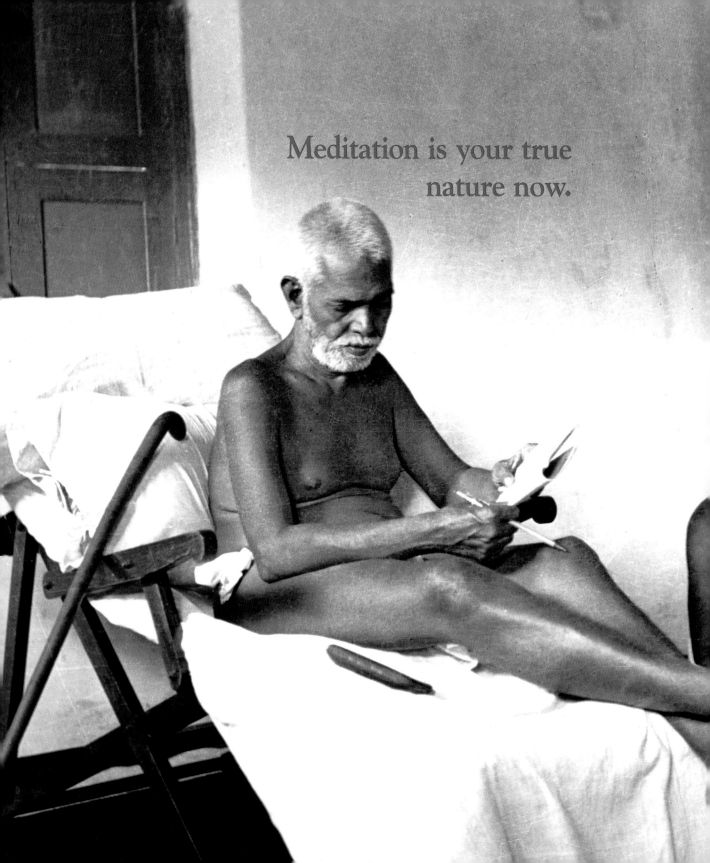

Meditation is your true
nature now.

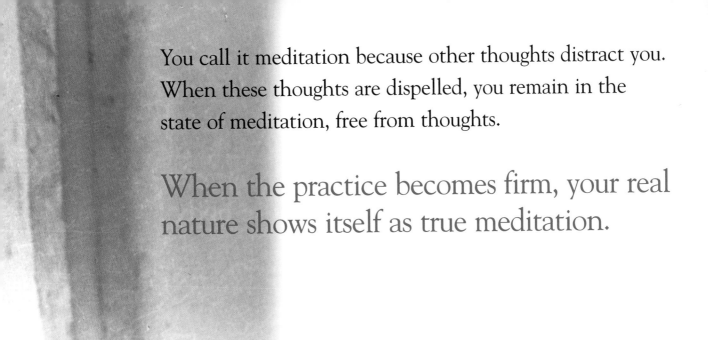

You call it meditation because other thoughts distract you.
When these thoughts are dispelled, you remain in the
state of meditation, free from thoughts.

When the practice becomes firm, your real
nature shows itself as true meditation.

When meditation is well-established,
it cannot be given up.
It will go on automatically, even
when you are engaged in work
or play. It will persist in sleep, too.

Meditation must become
so deep-rooted that it
will be natural
to one.

Birth and death pertain only to the body . . .

. . . they are superimposed on the Self, giving rise to the delusion that birth and death relate to the Self.

If one dies while still alive, one
need not grieve over another's death.

Discover the undying Self and be immortal and happy.

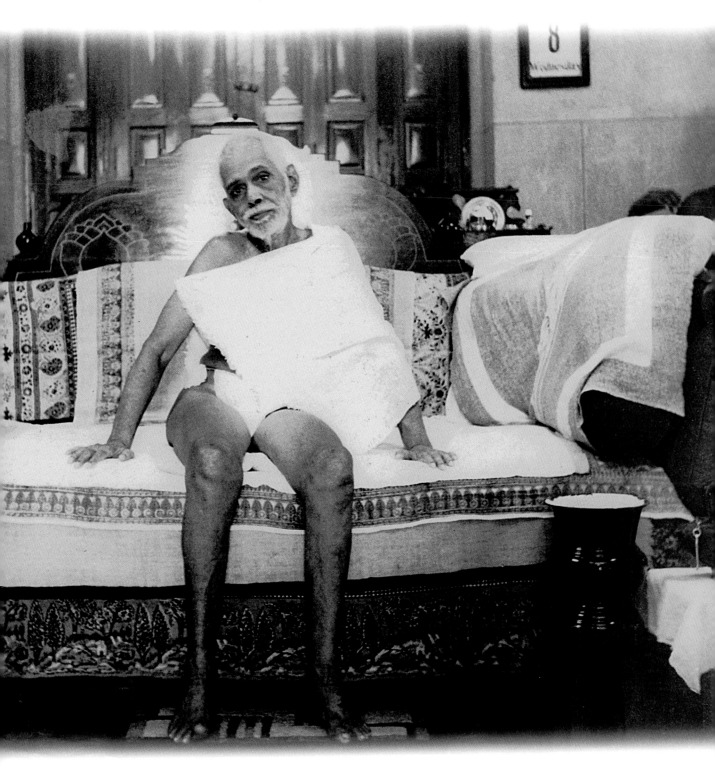

Why do you worry about life and death?

Deathlessness is our real nature.
The real "I" exists here and now.

There is neither creation nor destruction,
neither destiny nor free will, neither
path nor achievement.
This is the final truth.

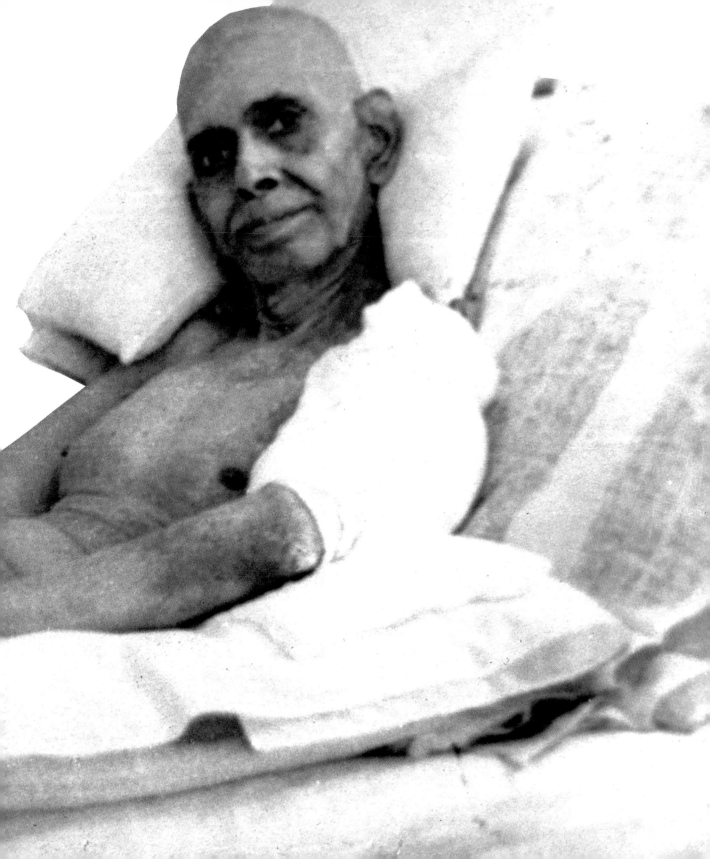

Referenced Works

A *Sadhu's Reminiscences*, by A. W. Chadwick

Day by Day with Bhagavan, Devaraja Mudaliar, compiler

Letters from Sri Ramanasramam, by Suri Nagamma

Sri Ramana the Sage of Arunagiri, G. R. Subbaramayya, compiler

Talks with Ramana Maharshi, Munagala S. Venkataramiah, compiler

The Collected Works of Ramana Maharshi, Arthur Osborne, editor

The Teachings of Ramana Maharshi, Arthur Osborne, editor

Upadesa Saram, by Ramana Maharshi

Who Am I?, by Ramana Maharshi

Photo References

Page

Photo Credits

Matthew Greenblatt: 17, 18, 20-21, 29, 34-35, 38, 44, 54, 73, 74, 83, 84, 90-91, 100, 104-105, 111
Anne Newberg: 62-63, 68-69, 89
Dorothy Tanus: 48-49, 52, 95, 103
Sri Ramanasramam: All photos of Sri Ramana Maharshi

InnerDirections
P U B L I S H I N G

InnerDirections Publishing is the imprint of the Inner Directions Foundation, a nonprofit organization dedicated to exploring self-discovery and awakening to one's essential nature.

We publish distinctive book and video titles that express the heart of authentic spirituality. Each of our titles presents an original perspective, with a clarity and insight that can only come from the experience of ultimate reality. These unique publications communicate the immediacy of *That* which is eternal and infinite within us: the nondualistic ground from which religions and spiritual traditions arise.

Inner Directions depends upon the support of people like you—friends who recognize the merit of an organization whose sole purpose is to disseminate works of enduring spiritual value. To receive our catalog or to find out how you can help sponsor an upcoming publishing project, call, write, or e-mail:

Inner Directions
P. O. Box 130070
Carlsbad, CA 92013

Tel: 760 599-4075
Fax: 760 599-4076
Orders: 800 545-9118

E-mail: mail@InnerDirections.org
Website: www.InnerDirections.org